MW01134039

AMAZING & INSPIRING
REAL LIFE
DOG HEROES
TRUE STORIES
FOR KIDS AND FAMILIES

BY
ANTHONY RIPLEY

1st edition 2023

This book *is dedicated to all dogs, and the humans that love them.*

— Anthony Ripley

Welcome to "Real Life Hero Dogs: True Stories for Kids and Families." In this book, you will meet some of the bravest dogs in the world, who have gone above and beyond to help their humans and other animals in need.

From search and rescue dogs to police dogs, from therapy dogs to guide dogs, these four-legged heroes have proven time and time again that they are much more than just pets. Each story will inspire you and show you the incredible bond that can exist between humans and their furry companions. Get ready to be amazed and inspired by these incredible canine heroes!

Table of Contents

Table of Contents

Balto

The Brave Sled Dog Who Saved a Town

    In the winter of 1925, a deadly outbreak of diphtheria threatened the remote town of Nome, Alaska. The only way to save the town was to deliver life-saving serum from Anchorage, Alaska, to Nome. But the town was located hundreds of miles away, and the only way to get the serum there was by dog sled. That's when Balto, a heroic sled dog, stepped up to the challenge and led a team of sled dogs on a dangerous 650-mile journey through blizzard conditions to deliver the serum and save the town.

Balto was a Siberian Husky who was born in Nome, Alaska, in 1919. He was owned by a Norwegian immigrant named Gunnar Kaasen, who was a dog sled racer. Balto was a strong and fearless dog who was known for his endurance and determination.

In 1925, a diphtheria outbreak struck the town of Nome. Diphtheria is a serious bacterial infection that can cause breathing problems and heart failure. There was no cure for the disease at the time, and it was spreading quickly through the town. The only hope was to get serum from Anchorage, Alaska, to Nome as quickly as possible.

The problem was that Nome was located hundreds of miles away, and there was no road that connected the town to the rest of Alaska. The only way to get the serum to Nome was by dog sled. A relay of dog sled teams was organized to transport the serum from Anchorage to Nome, with each team covering a portion of the journey.

Balto was part of the last team of sled dogs that was tasked with delivering the serum to Nome. The team left Nome on January 27, 1925, and was led by a musher named Gunnar Kaasen. The team faced blizzard conditions and temperatures as low as -50 degrees Fahrenheit. The journey was treacherous, with deep snowdrifts, ice-covered rivers, and rocky terrain.

Despite the dangers, Balto and the other sled dogs pushed on, carrying the precious serum that could save the lives of many people in Nome. Balto, in particular, was a strong and fearless leader who never gave up. He led the team through the blizzard conditions and over treacherous terrain, with his keen sense of direction guiding the team through the worst of the storm.

The team arrived in Nome on February 2, 1925, after traveling over 650 miles in just five and a half days. The serum was quickly distributed to the people in Nome, and many lives were saved as a result. The town was saved from the deadly outbreak, and Balto became a hero.

Balto's heroism was celebrated across the country. He and Gunnar Kaasen were invited to New York City, where they were welcomed as heroes. Balto even received a medal from the city of New York in recognition of his bravery and determination.

Today, Balto is remembered as a symbol of courage and determination. His story has been retold in books, movies, and television shows, and he is still celebrated as a hero in Alaska and across the country. In fact, a statue of Balto was erected in Central Park in New York City in 1926, and it still stands there today.

Balto's legacy also lives on through sled dog racing. Dog sled racing has become a popular sport in Alaska and other parts of the world, and it continues to be a testament to the endurance and strength of sled dogs like Balto.

Stubby

The Brave Pit Bull Who Served in WW1

During World War I, a brave little pit bull mix named Stubby served alongside the U.S. Army in the trenches of France. Stubby was a hero who saved lives, captured enemy soldiers, and brought comfort to wounded soldiers. In this article, we'll explore the amazing story of Stubby, the dog who became a legend of the Great War.

Stubby was found wandering the streets of New Haven, Connecticut in 1917, where he was taken in by Private J. Robert Conroy of the 102nd Infantry Regiment. Conroy was training with his unit at Yale University, and Stubby became the regiment's unofficial mascot.

When the regiment was deployed to France, Conroy snuck Stubby onto the ship, and he became a member of the 26th Yankee Division. Stubby quickly became a favorite among the soldiers, and he was given the rank of Sergeant, becoming the first dog to be given military rank in the United States Army.

Stubby's service in the war was impressive. He was trained to detect incoming gas attacks, and he would alert the soldiers by barking and running to the nearest gas mask station. He was also trained to locate wounded soldiers on the battlefield, and he would comfort them until medics arrived.

In one instance, Stubby even saved the life of his owner, Private Conroy. Conroy was injured in a gas attack, and Stubby dragged him to safety. Stubby's bravery and loyalty earned him a special place in the hearts of the soldiers.

Stubby's most famous act of heroism came when he helped capture a German spy. The spy was trying to map out the positions of the Allied troops, but Stubby detected him and attacked him, biting him on the leg and holding him down until the soldiers could capture him.

Stubby became a legend among the soldiers, and he was featured in many newspapers and magazines. He even met several high-ranking officials, including President Woodrow Wilson and General John J. Pershing.

After the war, Stubby returned home a hero. He was given a hero's welcome, and he was even invited to lead a parade in New York City. Stubby went on to become a celebrity, appearing in several movies and performing in circuses across the country.

Stubby's legacy lives on today. He is remembered as a brave and loyal dog who served his country with distinction. In fact, Stubby's story inspired the creation of the U.S. Army's K-9 Corps, which trains dogs to serve in the military.

Today, there are many ways to honor Stubby's memory. The Connecticut State Library has a collection of Stubby's artifacts, including his medals and his uniform. The Smithsonian National Museum of American History also has a display honoring Stubby's service in the war.

In conclusion, Stubby was a brave and loyal dog who served in World War I and became a legend of the Great War. His heroism and loyalty earned him a special place in the hearts of the soldiers he served with. Stubby's legacy lives on as an inspiration to all who serve their country with bravery and dedication.

Chips

The Brave War Dog

Have you ever heard of Chips, the brave war dog who helped his army unit during World War II? Chips was a German Shepherd-Collie-Siberian Husky mix who served in the United States Army during the war. He was a loyal and brave companion who helped capture 10 Italian soldiers and alerted his handlers to hidden enemies.

Chips was born in Pleasantville, New York, in 1940. His owner, Edward J. Wren, was an army private who enlisted Chips in the army in 1942. Chips was sent to basic training in Fort Dix, New Jersey, where he quickly proved himself to be a smart and talented dog. He was trained to be a sentry dog, which meant he would help guard the military base from any threats.

After his training was completed, Chips was sent to North Africa to join the Allied Forces in their fight against the Axis Powers. He was assigned to the 3rd Infantry Division and quickly became an important member of his unit.

In 1943, Chips and his unit were sent on a mission to invade the Axis-held beach in Sicily, Italy. The mission was a dangerous one, as the Axis Powers had heavily fortified the beach with mines and other traps. Chips and his handler, Private John P. Rowell, were part of the first wave of troops to hit the beach.

As soon as Chips landed on the beach, he sprang into action. He immediately started sniffing out hidden enemy soldiers and mines. Chips was so good at his job that he quickly alerted his handlers to the presence of 10 Italian soldiers who had been hiding in a nearby pillbox.

Chips did not hesitate to attack the enemy soldiers. He charged into the pillbox and tackled the first soldier he saw. His handlers quickly followed, and together they captured the 10 Italian soldiers without any casualties. Chips was praised for his bravery and received a Silver Star, a Purple Heart, and other commendations for his actions.

Chips was not done yet, though. He continued to serve with his unit in the North African and European campaigns. He helped sniff out mines, locate hidden enemy soldiers, and even helped carry messages between units.

One time, Chips was wounded when he ran over a live mine. He was hit in the chest and the muzzle, but he refused to give up. He continued to serve with his unit, even though he was wounded.

Chips became a beloved member of his unit. He was known for his bravery, loyalty, and intelligence. His handlers even taught him a few tricks, like how to salute and how to carry messages in his mouth.

After the war, Chips returned to the United States and was discharged from the army. He went to live with his owner, Edward J. Wren, in Pleasantville, New York. Chips became a celebrity, and his story was featured in newspapers and on the radio.

Chips died in 1946, but his memory lives on. He was a true hero who helped his unit during one of the most difficult times in history. His bravery and loyalty inspired many people, and he is still remembered as one of the greatest war dogs in history.

Chips' story is a great reminder of the important role that animals can play in our lives. Dogs, cats, and other animals have been serving humans for thousands of years, and their loyalty and bravery have helped save countless lives. Chips was a true hero who will always be remembered for his incredible contributions to Allied Forces during World War II.

Buddy

*The First Seeing Eye Dog in the
United States*

Buddy was a German Shepherd who changed the lives of many people with visual impairments. He became the first seeing eye dog in the United States and helped his owner, Morris Frank, navigate his daily life after he became blind. Buddy was a loyal and intelligent companion who inspired the creation of the Seeing Eye, the first guide dog school in the United States.

Morris Frank was born in Philadelphia, Pennsylvania, in 1903. When he was just 16 months old, he contracted an illness that left him blind. Despite his blindness, Morris was determined to live a full and independent life. He learned how to read Braille and attended school with sighted children.

As Morris grew older, he realized that he needed a way to navigate the world more independently. He heard about a school in Switzerland that was training dogs to guide people who were blind. Morris was intrigued and decided to go to Switzerland to learn more.

In Switzerland, Morris met Dorothy Harrison Eustis, who was the founder of the school that trained guide dogs. Eustis had been training German Shepherds to guide people who were blind since the early 1920s. She was impressed by Morris's determination and decided to train a dog for him.

Eustis chose a German Shepherd named Buddy for Morris. Buddy was a smart and affectionate dog who quickly bonded with Morris. Eustis trained Buddy to guide Morris safely through the streets, stop at curbs and stairs, and avoid obstacles like trees and traffic.

Morris and Buddy returned to the United States in 1928. They quickly became celebrities, and their story was featured in newspapers and on the radio. Morris started the Seeing Eye, which was the first guide dog school in the United States. He and Buddy traveled around the country to raise awareness about guide dogs and to encourage more people with visual impairments to use them.

Buddy was a great help to Morris. He guided him safely through the streets, helped him cross busy intersections, and even helped him find his way around new places. Buddy was also a great companion who provided Morris with love and companionship.

Buddy's success inspired many other people with visual impairments to get guide dogs. The Seeing Eye became a popular and successful guide dog school, and guide dogs became an important part of the lives of many people with visual impairments.

Buddy's legacy lives on today. Guide dogs are still used to help people with visual impairments navigate the world more independently. The Seeing Eye is still in operation and has trained over 17,000 guide dogs since it was founded.

Buddy's story is a great reminder of the important role that animals can play in our lives. Guide dogs, service dogs, and other animals have been helping humans for thousands of years, and their loyalty and intelligence have saved countless lives.

In addition to helping Morris Frank, Buddy also helped raise awareness about the capabilities of guide dogs. Before Buddy, there were no seeing eye dogs in the United States, and many people with visual impairments were unaware of the benefits of having a guide dog.

After Buddy and Morris returned to the United States, Morris founded the Seeing Eye, which is still in operation today. The Seeing Eye has trained thousands of guide dogs and has helped countless people with visual impairments live more independent lives.

Guide dogs are trained to do many things, such as helping their owners navigate busy streets, avoiding obstacles, and finding objects. They are also trained to be calm and obedient in a variety of situations, which makes them great companions for people with visual impairments.

Guide dogs also provide their handlers with emotional support and companionship. Many people with visual impairments feel isolated and alone, but guide dogs provide them with a loyal and affectionate companion who is always there to help.

Apollo

The Brave Rescue Dog of 9/11

Apollo was a German Shepherd who was born in 1992 in the Netherlands. He was trained as a search and rescue dog and worked alongside the New York City Police Department (NYPD) in search and rescue efforts after the terrorist attacks on September 11, 2001. Apollo's heroic efforts helped to find survivors in the rubble and bring closure to families who had lost loved ones.

On September 11, 2001, terrorists attacked the World Trade Center in New York City, causing the collapse of the twin towers. The attack left many people trapped in the rubble. The NYPD immediately launched a search and rescue effort to find survivors.

Apollo was one of the many dogs that were brought in to help with the search and rescue effort. He and his handler, Peter Davis, were assigned to the task of searching for survivors in the rubble of the World Trade Center.

Apollo and Davis worked tirelessly for weeks, searching through the rubble for signs of life. They would work for hours at a time, navigating through the debris and rubble, looking for any sign of a survivor. Appollo's sense of smell was critical in locating survivors who might otherwise have been missed by the search teams.

Apollo was a trained search and rescue dog, and he was able to detect the scent of humans even when they were buried deep in the rubble. He was also trained to work in difficult conditions, such as in the dark or in areas with limited visibility. This made him a valuable asset to the search and rescue effort.

Apollo's work was not without danger. The rubble was unstable, and there was a risk of further collapse. Appollo and Davis had to be careful to navigate through the rubble without putting themselves in danger.

Despite the risks, Apollo and Davis continued to work tirelessly. Their efforts paid off when they located a survivor in the rubble. The survivor was a young woman who had been trapped for several days. Apollo's sense of smell had detected her scent, and he was able to lead the rescue workers to her location.

Apollo's heroism was celebrated across the country. He and Davis were invited to the White House, where they were honored for their bravery and dedication. Apollo also received several awards, including the Dickin Medal, which is the highest award that can be given to an animal for bravery in war.

Apollo's work at Ground Zero was not just about finding survivors. It was also about bringing closure to families who had lost loved ones in the attacks. Apollo and the other search and rescue dogs were able to locate many bodies, which helped families to find closure and say goodbye to their loved ones.

After his work at Ground Zero, Apollo retired from the NYPD and spent the rest of his life living with Davis. He became an ambassador for search and rescue dogs, helping to raise awareness about their important work.

Today, Apollo is remembered as a hero of 9/11. His bravery and dedication helped to save lives and bring closure to families who had lost loved ones. His legacy continues to inspire others to work for the greater good and to never give up in the face of adversity.

In conclusion, Apollo was a brave and determined search and rescue dog who worked alongside the NYPD in the aftermath of the 9/11 terrorist attacks. His heroism and dedication helped to find survivors and bring closure to families who had lost loved ones. Apollo's legacy lives on as an inspiration to others to work for the greater good and to never give up in the face of adversity.

Bretagne

The Heroic Golden Retriever

On September 11, 2001, a group of terrorists attacked the World Trade Center in New York City. The attack caused the collapse of the Twin Towers, leaving thousands of people trapped in the rubble. In the aftermath of the tragedy, rescue workers from all over the country came to help search for survivors. Among them was a brave Golden Retriever named Bretagne.

Bretagne was just two years old when she was trained as a search and rescue dog. She was partnered with a firefighter named Denise Corliss, and together they worked for the Cy-Fair Volunteer Fire Department in Texas. Bretagne was trained to find people in all kinds of situations, from natural disasters to terrorist attacks.

When the call came to help search for survivors at Ground Zero, Bretagne and Denise were among the first to respond. They traveled to New York City on September 17th, just six days after the attacks. Bretagne was one of only about 300 search and rescue dogs who worked at the site, and she quickly became a favorite among the rescue workers.

Bretagne and Denise worked long hours, searching through the rubble for any sign of life. Bretagne was trained to detect the scent of humans, and she used her powerful nose to sniff out any survivors who might be trapped under the rubble. She worked tirelessly, even when she became tired and hungry.

One of Bretagne's most memorable moments at Ground Zero came when she was able to help comfort a firefighter who had lost his colleagues in the attacks. The firefighter was sitting on the curb, crying, and Bretagne went over to him and put her head in his lap. The firefighter stroked her fur and talked to her, and it helped him to feel a little better.

Bretagne and Denise worked at Ground Zero for 10 days, until all hope of finding survivors was lost. Despite the difficult and dangerous conditions, Bretagne remained focused and determined throughout the search. She never lost her spirit or her love for her work.

After the search was over, Bretagne and Denise returned to Texas. Bretagne was hailed as a hero, and she received many awards and honors for her service at Ground Zero. She even had a birthday party in New York City in 2014, when she turned 15 years old.

Bretagne lived a long and happy life after her service at Ground Zero. She continued to work as a search and rescue dog, helping to find survivors in other disasters such as Hurricane Katrina. She also became a therapy dog, visiting schools and hospitals to bring comfort to people who were going through difficult times.

In 2016, Bretagne passed away at the age of 16. She was given a hero's farewell, with firefighters and other rescue workers lining the street to say goodbye. Bretagne was a hero, a friend, and a companion to many people, and she will always be remembered as a symbol of hope and courage in the face of tragedy.

Gander

The Brave Newfoundland Who Saved His Army Unit

Dogs have been loyal companions and protectors of humans for centuries. They have served in wars, helped people with disabilities, and even saved lives. Gander, a gentle giant Newfoundland, was one such heroic dog whose bravery and loyalty were recognized posthumously. He became a legend in the Canadian Armed Forces for his fearless actions during the Battle of Lye Mun in Hong Kong in 1941.

Gander was born in 1939 in a small town in Newfoundland, Canada. He was a big, friendly, and intelligent dog who loved children and was known to be a bit of a troublemaker. His owner, Harry Colebourn, was a soldier in the Canadian Army and had trained Gander to be his companion and guard dog. When Harry was deployed to England in 1940 to serve in World War II, he left Gander with the Royal Rifles of Canada, who were stationed in Newfoundland.

Gander quickly became the regimental mascot and was loved by all the soldiers. He was trained to follow orders and do his part in the war effort. In November 1941, the regiment was sent to Hong Kong to defend against the Japanese invasion. Gander was also deployed with the regiment as a mascot, but he quickly proved to be much more than that.

During the Battle of Lye Mun, the Japanese soldiers launched a surprise attack on the Canadian troops, who were caught off guard. Gander sprang into action and charged at the enemy, barking and biting at them. He grabbed a live grenade that had been thrown by the Japanese soldiers and ran towards them, sacrificing his own life to protect his unit. The grenade exploded, killing Gander instantly, but his actions saved the lives of many Canadian soldiers who were in the vicinity.

Gander's heroic actions were not forgotten by the soldiers who witnessed his bravery. His story was passed down through the generations and became a symbol of courage and loyalty in the Canadian Armed Forces. In 2000, Gander was posthumously awarded the Dickin Medal, the animal equivalent of the Victoria Cross, for his bravery and devotion to duty.

Today, Gander's legacy lives on in his hometown of Gander, Newfoundland. The local airport was named after him, and a statue of him was erected in the town square to honor his bravery. The Royal Rifles of Canada also established the Gander Memorial Award, which is given to a Canadian who has performed an act of valor, bravery, or devotion to duty.

Gander was a gentle giant who touched the hearts of everyone he met. His selfless actions during the Battle of Lye Mun were a testament to his loyalty, courage, and devotion to duty. He will always be remembered as a true hero, who gave his life to protect his fellow soldiers.

Roselle

The Guide Dog Who Saved Lives on 9/11

On September 11, 2001, the world watched in horror as the Twin Towers of the World Trade Center in New York City were attacked by terrorists. It was a day that changed the lives of millions of people forever. But amidst the chaos and destruction, there were heroes who emerged. One of them was a guide dog named Roselle.

Roselle was a three-year-old Labrador Retriever who had been trained as a guide dog for the blind. Her owner, Michael Hingson, was a sales manager for a computer company and had been blind since birth. He and Roselle had been working together for just over a year, and their bond was strong.

On the morning of September 11, Michael and Roselle were at their office on the 78th floor of Tower One of the World Trade Center. They were working when suddenly they heard a loud explosion. The building shook, and the lights went out. Michael knew immediately that something was wrong.

Roselle, however, remained calm. She sensed that her owner was scared and anxious, and she knew that it was her job to take care of him. She guided Michael to the stairwell, and together they began their descent down the stairs.

As they made their way down the stairs, they encountered many other people who were trying to escape the building. Some of them were injured, and others were disoriented and confused. But Roselle remained focused on her job, guiding Michael and keeping him safe.

The journey down the stairs was long and difficult. The air was thick with smoke and dust, and the stairwell was crowded and chaotic. But Roselle never wavered. She led Michael through the darkness, down the stairs, and out of the building.

When they emerged from the building, they found themselves in a street that was covered in debris and dust. People were running and screaming, and emergency vehicles were rushing to the scene. But Roselle remained calm. She led Michael away from the chaos and to a safe place where they could rest and wait for help.

Michael and Roselle had survived one of the worst terrorist attacks in history. They had made it out of the building alive, thanks in large part to Roselle's bravery and determination.

After the attack, Michael and Roselle became celebrities. They were featured in news articles and television shows, and Michael even wrote a book about their experience. But despite all the attention, Roselle remained the same loyal and devoted guide dog that she had always been. She continued to work with Michael and to guide him through his daily life.

Sadly, Roselle passed away in 2011 at the age of 13. But her legacy lives on. She was a hero on September 11, 2001, and her courage and dedication continue to inspire people today.

In honor of Roselle's bravery, a statue of her was unveiled in the lobby of the 9/11 Museum in New York City in 2017. The statue depicts Roselle leading Michael down the stairs of the World Trade Center on the day of the attack.

The story of Roselle is a testament to the bond between humans and animals. She was more than just a guide dog; she was a loyal companion, a protector, and a hero. Her bravery and dedication saved lives on the day of the 9/11 attacks, and her memory will continue to inspire people for years to come.

The story of Roselle and Michael is a powerful reminder of the bravery and resilience of the human spirit. Despite the tragedy and chaos of that fateful day, Roselle remained focused on her job and helped her owner escape to safety. Her actions saved lives, and her legacy will continue to inspire people.

Zanjeer

The Heroic Bomb-Sniffing Labrador

Zanjeer was a Labrador Retriever who worked with the Mumbai Police and helped detect 3,329 kilograms of explosive material, thus saving countless lives in India. But before we talk about Zanjeer's heroic deeds, let's learn a little about his life.

Zanjeer was born in 1992 in a small village in Hyderabad, India. He was trained by the police to become a bomb-sniffing dog and was soon sent to Mumbai to join the police force. His first assignment was the bomb squad.

Zanjeer quickly became an indispensable member of the bomb squad. He was so good at his job that he was often called upon to work on high-risk operations. He could sniff out even the smallest traces of explosive material, which helped the police prevent numerous terror attacks.

One of Zanjeer's most notable accomplishments was during the Mumbai serial blasts in 1993. Zanjeer was only a year old at the time, but he played a crucial role in finding and defusing several bombs. His efforts helped save countless lives, and he was hailed as a hero by the people of Mumbai.

Over the years, Zanjeer continued to work tirelessly with the police. He was responsible for detecting over 3,329 kilograms of explosive material during his service, which is an incredible feat.

But Zanjeer wasn't just a hardworking police dog. He was also a beloved member of the police force and the community. Zanjeer would often visit schools and hospitals to interact with children and bring a smile to their faces. He even appeared in a Bollywood movie!

In 2000, Zanjeer retired from the police force after eight years of dedicated service. He lived out his remaining years with his handler, Sub-Inspector Gajanan Kabdule. Zanjeer passed away in 2000, but his legacy lived on.

In recognition of his service and bravery, Zanjeer was posthumously awarded the Ashoka Chakra, India's highest peacetime military decoration, in 2000. He was the first and only police dog to receive this honor.

Zanjeer's heroic deeds and legacy serve as an inspiration to all of us. He showed us that with hard work, dedication, and a bit of love, we can all make a difference in the world.

So the next time you see a police dog on the street or on TV, remember Zanjeer and all the other brave dogs who work tirelessly to keep us safe. And who knows, maybe you'll even be inspired to make a difference in the world yourself.

Sinbad

The Heroic Coastguard Dog of WWII

Sinbad was a four-legged hero who served in the U.S. Coast Guard during World War II. This brave dog was known for his incredible senses and quick reflexes that helped his unit to be aware of incoming aircraft and mines. Let's dive into the story of Sinbad, the fearless Coast Guard dog.

Sinbad was a mix of a German Shepherd and Alaskan Husky breed. He was initially adopted by a Coast Guard seaman named A.A. "Blackie" Roth in

1937, who took him onboard the USCGC Campbell, a Coast Guard Cutter. Roth's intent was to have Sinbad as a pet, but soon, the dog became an integral part of the crew. Sinbad's ability to detect incoming aircraft and mines was unmatched, and the crew started relying on him heavily.

In his first year onboard, Sinbad accompanied the ship on many patrols, and soon he became a favorite amongst the crew. Sinbad was not only an expert in detecting incoming danger but also had a friendly and playful personality. The crew adored him, and he quickly became an integral part of the ship's daily routines.

During one of their voyages, Sinbad saved the day by detecting a bomb. The ship was sailing in the North Atlantic Ocean, and suddenly, Sinbad started barking and growling. His behavior was unusual and caught the attention of the crew. They realized that the ship had sailed into a minefield, and Sinbad had detected a mine. The crew immediately took evasive action and were able to avoid the mine, thanks to Sinbad's keen senses. This incident earned Sinbad a promotion to Chief Dog.

Sinbad's duty wasn't just to protect the ship from mines and bombs; he was also an excellent morale booster. The crewmembers would often play with him during their downtime, and he would playfully chase them around the deck. Sinbad also had a particular fondness for the sailors' hats, and he would often playfully grab them and run away. He became a constant source of entertainment and love for the sailors on the ship.

Sinbad continued his service to the USCGC Campbell until 1945, when he retired from active duty. However, his fame continued to grow, and he became a sensation amongst the US Coast Guard veterans. Sinbad retired with his handler Blackie Roth, and the two of them lived together until the dog's death in 1951.

Sinbad's heroic deeds did not go unnoticed, and he was awarded many honors and recognitions. In 1943, he was awarded the American Defense Service Medal for his contributions to the Coast Guard. In 1946, he was awarded the honor of "Permanent Chief Petty Officer" by the US Coast Guard, making him the only dog in Coast Guard history to receive this honor. The crewmembers of the USCGC Campbell also raised a statue in his honor, which stands to this day in the Coast Guard museum in New London, Connecticut.

In conclusion, Sinbad was a remarkable dog who served his country with utmost dedication and loyalty. He was not just a pet but an integral part of the USCGC Campbell's crew, and his keen senses saved many lives. He was a source of constant entertainment and love for his sailors, and his personality was infectious. Even today, he is remembered as a hero who made a significant contribution to the US Coast Guard's history.

Ludivine

The Unlikely Marathon Runner

Ludivine was a curious and adventurous bloodhound who lived in Elkmont, Alabama. She loved nothing more than exploring the outdoors and chasing after scents. One day, she stumbled upon something she had never seen before: a marathon.

It was a cold January day in 2016, and the starting line of the Trackless Train Trek Half Marathon was set up just a few blocks from

Ludivine's house. As she sniffed around, she found herself drawn to the excitement of the runners and decided to join in on the fun.

Without anyone realizing it, Ludivine snuck into the crowd of runners and took off with them at the sound of the starting gun. She didn't have a bib number or a human companion, but that didn't stop her from running alongside the other athletes.

At first, some of the runners thought it was funny to see a dog keeping up with them, but as they progressed through the course, Ludivine's determination and stamina impressed everyone. She ran through neighborhoods, fields, and forests, stopping only to drink from puddles or chase after a squirrel or two.

As word of the unexpected participant in the race spread, Ludivine's owner April Hamlin was shocked to find out her dog was out and about on the racecourse. "My first reaction was that I was embarrassed and worried that she had caused a problem," Hamlin said in an interview with Runner's World. "But when I saw the pictures of her at the finish line and heard the story of how she did, I was proud of her."

Ludivine crossed the finish line in seventh place, with an impressive time of 1 hour and 32 minutes. Her unexpected feat quickly became a sensation, and she was dubbed "The Hound Who Ran a Half Marathon" by the media.

In recognition of her achievement, Ludivine was awarded a well-deserved medal for completing the race. Her medal featured a picture of a bloodhound and the words "Trackless Train Trek Half Marathon," making her the only non-human participant in the race to receive one.

Ludivine's fame quickly spread beyond Elkmont and even caught the attention of international media outlets. She was featured on news programs and in newspapers across the world, becoming a viral sensation.

But for Ludivine, the half marathon was just another adventure in her daily life. She continued to enjoy her daily walks and runs, always eager to explore and find new scents. Her owners were surprised by the sudden fame their dog had garnered, but they were happy that she had brought some joy and inspiration to so many people.

Ludivine's story shows that sometimes, the most unexpected things can happen, and it's important to always be open to new experiences. Her determination and spirit have inspired many people to never give up on their dreams, no matter how impossible they may seem.

As for Ludivine, she's still enjoying her life as a curious and adventurous bloodhound, always eager to explore the world around her. Who knows what other unexpected adventures she may have in store for us in the future?

Figo

The Brave Guide Dog Who Saved His Owner's Life

Figo was a brave and loyal Golden Retriever who put his life on the line to protect his owner, Audrey Stone. Audrey is visually impaired and relies on Figo to guide her through her daily life. Together, they were an unstoppable team.

One day, while crossing the street, Audrey and Figo were suddenly struck by a school bus. In an instant, Figo knew he had to act fast. He leaped in front of the bus, taking the brunt of the impact and shielding Audrey from harm.

Despite his injuries, Figo refused to leave Audrey's side. He stayed by her side, licking her face and comforting her until paramedics arrived to take them both to the hospital. Audrey suffered a broken ankle and some bumps and bruises, but she was alive and safe thanks to Figo's heroic actions.

News of Figo's bravery quickly spread, and people from all over the world were amazed by his selflessness and courage. The American Kennel Club even awarded him with their 2016 Award for Canine Excellence (ACE) for his heroic actions.

Figo was no stranger to the limelight, though. In fact, he and Audrey had been a well-known duo in their town for years. They could often be seen walking together, Figo guiding Audrey with ease and grace.

Figo was trained as a guide dog by the Guide Dog Foundation for the Blind, an organization that helps people who are visually impaired or blind navigate their daily lives with the help of guide dogs like Figo. The foundation provides extensive training and support to both the dogs and their owners, ensuring that they are both well-prepared for their lives together.

Guide dogs like Figo are trained to perform a wide range of tasks, from leading their owners around obstacles to alerting them to changes in elevation or uneven terrain. They are also trained to respond to vocal and hand commands, so their owners can communicate with them effectively.

In addition to their practical skills, guide dogs also provide their owners with a sense of independence, confidence, and companionship. For many people who are visually impaired or blind, having a guide dog by their side is a life-changing experience.

Figo was a shining example of what a guide dog can do. He not only helped Audrey navigate her daily life, but he also risked his own safety to protect her when she was in danger. His bravery and devotion inspired people all over the world and reminded us of the incredible bond between humans and animals.

Figo lived out the rest of his days with Audrey, by her side and always ready to help her in any way he could. He may have been just a dog, but to Audrey and to all those whose lives he touched, he was a true hero.

Hachiko

The Loyal Dog Who Never Gave Up

Dogs are known to be loyal creatures, but few can match the loyalty of Hachiko, a Japanese Akita who became famous for his unrelenting devotion to his owner.

Hachiko's story began in 1924 when he was brought to Tokyo by his owner, Professor Hidesaburo Ueno, a professor at the University of Tokyo. The professor and Hachiko quickly developed a close bond, and the dog would accompany his owner to the Shibuya Train Station every morning and wait patiently for him to return in the evening.

This routine continued for a little over a year until one day in May 1925, when Professor Ueno suffered a stroke while at work and passed away. When Hachiko arrived at the train station that evening and saw that his beloved owner was not there, he refused to leave the station and spent the night there, waiting for his owner to return.

The next day, Hachiko returned to the station at the same time as he had every day with his owner and waited patiently for his return. But the professor never came. Despite this, Hachiko continued to return to the station every day at the same time and wait for his owner's return, even after several weeks had passed.

Hachiko's loyalty and devotion did not go unnoticed, and soon he became a familiar sight to commuters passing through Shibuya Station. Some would stop to pet him, and others would offer him food and water, but nothing could deter him from his daily routine.

As time went by, Hachiko became a symbol of loyalty and devotion in Japan. His story was featured in newspapers and magazines, and people from all over the country began to hear about the dog who never gave up on his owner.

Hachiko's unwavering loyalty continued for over nine years, until his death in 1935. During this time, he had become a fixture at the station and had captured the hearts of the Japanese people. After his death, a statue was erected in his honor at Shibuya Station, and it still stands there today, a testament to his loyalty and devotion.

Hachiko's story has inspired countless people, and it continues to be a source of fascination and inspiration for many. In fact, in recent years, his story has been retold in movies, books, and even an anime series.

But beyond inspiring people, Hachiko's story also teaches us valuable lessons about loyalty, devotion, and perseverance. Even when faced with adversity and loss, Hachiko refused to give up on his owner, and his unwavering loyalty became a symbol of hope and inspiration for many.

So, the next time you see a dog waiting patiently for its owner, remember the story of Hachiko and the incredible loyalty and devotion that he showed to his owner. And perhaps, you too will be inspired by his story to be more loyal, more devoted, and more determined in your own life.

Smoky

One Brave Yorkie

    Meet Smoky, the brave Yorkshire Terrier who served in World War II and became a hero. Smoky wasn't just any dog - she was small, fearless, and smart. She helped the soldiers in the Philippines lay communication wires that were essential for keeping the troops connected and informed during the war. Her courage and quick thinking saved many lives, and she became a beloved mascot of the American soldiers.

Smoky was found by an American soldier named Bill Wynne in a foxhole in New Guinea. She was sick and tiny, but Bill took care of her and nursed her back to health. Smoky became Bill's constant companion and best friend. When Bill was transferred to the Philippines, he didn't want to leave Smoky behind. He convinced his commanding officer to let him take Smoky with him, and she became the mascot of the troops.

During the war, communication was a critical factor for the soldiers' success. The troops had to lay communication wires to keep in touch with headquarters. It was a dangerous job that required crawling through tiny pipes and tunnels. This is where Smoky came in. She was small enough to crawl through these spaces, and she didn't mind the loud noises or the dark, cramped conditions.

Smoky's service in the war wasn't easy. She traveled in a backpack, and the soldiers would lower her down into tunnels and pipes. She had to endure the same dangers as the soldiers, including gunfire and explosions. Despite these challenges, Smoky persevered and helped the soldiers lay the wires.

One of the most remarkable things about Smoky was her intelligence. She was trained to perform tasks that were beyond the abilities of other dogs. Smoky could communicate with hand signals, and she was trained to identify different sounds, including incoming enemy planes. Her intelligence made her a valuable asset to the troops.

Smoky's bravery and intelligence were put to the test when she had to help out in the hospital. One day, a soldier was badly injured and needed surgery, but the hospital didn't have any medical supplies. Smoky was the only one who could help. She crawled through a pipe carrying a surgical tube with a wire attached to it. The doctors used the wire to perform the surgery on the soldier, and his life was saved. Smoky's quick thinking and bravery saved a life.

After the war, Smoky returned home with Bill, but her service didn't go unnoticed. She became famous for her bravery and was featured in newspapers and magazines. She was even awarded a medal for her service. Smoky became a celebrity, and she was featured on television shows and traveled around the country to meet with her fans.

Smoky's legacy lives on today. Her story has inspired many people, and she is remembered as a hero of the war. Smoky showed that even the smallest creatures can make a big difference. Her bravery, intelligence, and loyalty are qualities that we can all strive to have.

In conclusion, Smoky, the Yorkshire Terrier, was a hero of World War II. She helped lay communication wires in the Philippines, saved countless lives, and became a beloved mascot of the American soldiers. Smoky's bravery, intelligence, and loyalty inspire us today, and her story reminds us that even the smallest creatures can make a big difference.

Salty

Hero of Hurricane Katrina

Salty the golden retriever made a huge difference during Hurricane Katrina. Salty was a therapy dog who helped comfort and support people who were displaced by the storm. Her kind nature and comforting presence helped many people during a very difficult time.

Salty was born in 2003 and was trained as a therapy dog when she was just a puppy. She was trained to provide emotional support to people in hospitals, nursing homes, and schools. Salty had a very calm and friendly personality that made her a great therapy dog.

In August of 2005, Hurricane Katrina hit the Gulf Coast of the United States. The hurricane caused widespread destruction, and many people were left homeless and without basic necessities like food and water. The devastation was especially hard on children, who were scared and traumatized by the storm.

Salty's owner, Nancy Gassaway, knew that Salty could help. She contacted the American Red Cross and offered Salty's services as a therapy dog. The Red Cross accepted the offer, and Salty and Nancy headed to Louisiana to help.

When they arrived, Salty and Nancy were sent to a shelter in Baton Rouge. The shelter was filled with people who had lost everything in the storm. They were scared, tired, and didn't know what to do next. Salty's job was to provide comfort and support to these people.

At first, Salty was nervous. She had never been in a situation like this before, and there were so many people who needed her help. But Nancy encouraged her, and Salty quickly got to work. She went from person to person, wagging her tail and offering her paw for people to pet. Her gentle presence helped to calm the people in the shelter and gave them a sense of hope.

Salty's work at the shelter didn't go unnoticed. People started to talk about the "therapy dog" who was helping them through the storm. The local news even did a story on Salty, and she became a bit of a celebrity.

After a few days, Salty and Nancy were sent to New Orleans to help at a larger shelter. This shelter was even more chaotic than the first one. There were thousands of people crammed into the space, and it was hot and humid. But Salty didn't let that stop her. She went from person to person, offering her calming presence and wagging her tail. People would cry when they saw her, and then they would smile when she licked their face.

One of the most touching moments of Salty's time in New Orleans was when she met a little girl who had lost her entire family in the storm. The girl was alone and scared, and she didn't know what to do. Salty went right up to the girl and started licking her face. The girl smiled for the first time since the storm, and she hugged Salty tightly. Salty stayed with the girl for the rest of the day, providing her with the comfort and support she needed.

Salty worked tirelessly during her time in New Orleans. She would get up early in the morning and go to bed late at night. She was always ready to offer comfort to anyone who needed it. Her work helped to ease the pain of many people who were affected by Hurricane Katrina.

When Salty returned home, she was tired but happy. She had done important work, and she had made a difference in people's lives. Nancy was proud of Salty and knew that her work as a therapy dog would continue.

Salty's story is an example of the important work that therapy dogs do. These dogs are trained to provide emotional support to people who are going through difficult times. They offer comfort, love, and a sense of hope to people who need it most.

Cairo

The Canine Navy SEAL

Cairo was a Belgian Malinois, and he was one of the best military working dogs around. He worked alongside Navy SEALs, and his job was to keep them safe and help them complete their missions. In 2011, Cairo played a crucial role in a mission that would go down in history: the mission that led to the death of Osama bin Laden.

Cairo had been trained from a young age to be a military working dog. He was very smart and very athletic, which made him perfect for the job. His trainers worked with him every day to make sure he was ready for anything that might come his way.

Cairo's job was to search for explosives and other dangerous items. He was also trained to detect people who were hiding. This was especially important in the kinds of missions that the Navy SEALs were involved in. They often had to sneak into dangerous areas, and Cairo's job was to make sure they were safe.

In May of 2011, Cairo was called to duty for a very special mission. The mission was to capture or kill Osama bin Laden, who was the leader of a terrorist group called Al-Qaeda. The mission was extremely dangerous, and the Navy SEALs knew that they would need all the help they could get.

Cairo was flown to the site of the mission, which was in Pakistan. When he arrived, he was ready to go. He had been trained for missions like this, and he knew exactly what to do. Cairo was fitted with a special harness that allowed him to be lowered from a helicopter. This was how he would enter the compound where Osama bin Laden was hiding.

The mission was intense, and the Navy SEALs faced many challenges. They had to sneak into the compound without being detected, and they had to fight their way through a group of terrorists who were guarding the building. Cairo was with them every step of the way, sniffing out any danger and helping the SEALs stay safe.

Finally, after several hours, the Navy SEALs found Osama bin Laden. He was hiding in a room on the third floor of the building. The SEALs burst into the room, and there was a brief but intense firefight. In the chaos, Cairo did his job, barking and biting at anyone who posed a threat to the SEALs.

In the end, the mission was a success. Osama bin Laden was killed, and the Navy SEALs were able to complete their mission without any of their members being killed or seriously injured. Cairo played a crucial role in the mission, and he was hailed as a hero when he returned home.

Cairo's role in the mission that took down Osama bin Laden was just one of the many important jobs he did in his career as a military working dog. He was involved in many other missions, some of which were never made public. But the mission that made him famous was the one that proved just how valuable dogs can be in military operations.

Belgian Malinois like Cairo are still used by the military today. They are highly intelligent and very obedient, which makes them perfect for jobs like searching for explosives, detecting people, and providing support to soldiers. They are also very loyal, and they form strong bonds with the soldiers they work with.

Cairo was a brave and loyal military working dog who played a crucial role in one of the most important missions in modern history. He was a true hero, and he will always be remembered for his service and his bravery.

Lucca

The Bomb Sniffing Hero

Lucca was a German Shepherd, and she was one of the best bomb-sniffing dogs around. She served as a U.S. Marine Corps dog in both Iraq and Afghanistan, and she helped detect explosives that could have caused harm to many people.

Lucca was born in 2006 in Finland, and she was trained as a military working dog from a young age. Her training was rigorous, and it included learning how to detect a variety of explosives. She was also trained to work in a variety of environments, including urban and rural areas.

When Lucca was two years old, she was sent to the United States to begin her service with the U.S. Marine Corps. She was assigned to a handler named Gunnery Sergeant Chris Willingham, and the two of them quickly formed a strong bond. They trained together every day, and they became an unstoppable team.

Lucca's job was to search for explosives that had been hidden by insurgents. This was extremely dangerous work, as the explosives could be hidden anywhere. They could be buried underground, hidden in buildings, or even strapped to the bodies of suicide bombers.

Despite the danger, Lucca was very good at her job. She had an incredible sense of smell, and she was able to detect even the smallest amounts of explosives. This meant that she was able to find bombs that other methods might have missed.

Lucca's service in Iraq and Afghanistan was very challenging. She and her handler worked long hours, often in very hot and uncomfortable conditions. They also faced many dangers, including the threat of roadside bombs and other explosives.

Despite the challenges, Lucca never wavered in her dedication to her job. She was always focused and always ready to do her part to keep her fellow Marines safe. And her hard work paid off: during her six years of service, she helped detect more than 40 different explosive devices.

Lucca's most heroic moment came in March of 2012. She and her handler were on patrol in Afghanistan when they were hit by a roadside bomb. Lucca was badly injured, but she didn't give up. She continued to search for explosives, even though she was in pain and bleeding.

Her handler, Gunnery Sergeant Willingham, quickly realized that Lucca was in trouble. He rushed over to her and carried her to safety. She was then airlifted to a military hospital, where she received life-saving surgery.

Thanks to the quick thinking of her handler and the skill of the doctors who treated her, Lucca made a full recovery. She was eventually retired from military service and was adopted by her former handler, Gunnery Sergeant Willingham.

After her retirement, Lucca became a celebrity of sorts. She was featured in several news stories, and she even made an appearance on the "Today" show. People all over the world were inspired by her bravery and her dedication to her job.

Lucca's story is a testament to the incredible work that military working dogs do every day. They put their lives on the line to keep their fellow soldiers safe, and they do it with incredible bravery and dedication.

German Shepherds like Lucca are still used by the military today. They are highly intelligent and very obedient, which makes them perfect for jobs like searching for explosives and detecting people. They are also very loyal, and they form strong bonds with the soldiers they work with.

Chaser

The Dog With an Incredible Memory

Imagine having a dog who could learn the name of every single toy, ball, and bone in your house. That's exactly what Chaser, a Border Collie, was able to do! Chaser is one of the most amazing dogs in history, and her incredible ability to learn and remember the names of over 1,000 objects has made her famous around the world.

Chaser was born in South Carolina in 2004, and she was adopted by a woman named Dr. John Pilley when she was just eight weeks old. Dr. Pilley, who was a retired psychology professor, decided to use Chaser as a research subject to study the cognitive abilities of dogs.

At first, Dr. Pilley trained Chaser to recognize the names of just a few objects, like balls and frisbees. He would show Chaser a ball and say "ball," and then give her a treat. After repeating this process many times, Chaser started to understand that the word "ball" meant the object in front of her.

Dr. Pilley then started adding more objects to Chaser's training. He would show her a new toy, say the name of the toy, and then give her a treat. At first, Chaser struggled to remember all of the new names, but after a while, she was able to recognize and remember dozens of different objects.

As Chaser got better and better at learning new names, Dr. Pilley started to teach her more complex commands. For example, he would show her a group of objects and tell her to "find the frisbee" or "get the ball." Chaser was able to understand these commands and retrieve the correct object every time.

Dr. Pilley's training with Chaser was based on a technique called "associative learning," which is when an animal learns to associate a particular sound or word with a particular object or action. This technique has been used for centuries to train animals, but Dr. Pilley took it to a whole new level with Chaser.

Over time, Chaser's vocabulary grew and grew. She was able to learn the names of not just toys, but also different types of balls, ropes, and even specific articles of clothing. By the time she was six years old, Chaser had learned the names of over 1,000 objects!

Chaser's amazing ability to learn and remember names has made her a celebrity in the dog world. She has been featured on TV shows like 60 Minutes and The Today Show, and she has even written her own book called Chaser: Unlocking the Genius of the Dog Who Knows a Thousand Words.

But Chaser's skills aren't just impressive – they also have practical applications. For example, Chaser's ability to learn and remember the names of different objects could be used to train dogs for search and rescue missions. A dog that can recognize the names of specific items could be incredibly useful in finding missing people or locating specific objects in a disaster area.

Chaser has also inspired other researchers to study the cognitive abilities of dogs. Many scientists now believe that dogs are capable of much more complex thinking than we previously thought, and that they may even be able to understand abstract concepts like language and numbers.

Chaser passed away in 2019 at the age of 15, but her legacy lives on. She has inspired countless dog lovers around the world to explore the cognitive abilities of their own pets, and she has shown us just how amazing dogs can be.

So the next time you're playing with your dog, try teaching them the name of a new toy or object. Who knows – they might just surprise you with their own Chaser-like abilities!

Ben

The Heroic Border Collie

Ben was an ordinary Border Collie who loved to play and go on walks with his owner, Dave. But one day, Ben's life changed when he was called upon to do something extraordinary.

In May 2018, a hiker named Kate was reported missing in the Scottish Highlands. The area is known for its rugged terrain and unpredictable weather, and Kate had been hiking alone when she disappeared. The search for her was difficult, with teams of rescue workers and search dogs scouring the area for days.

That's when Ben and his owner, Dave, were called upon to join the search. Dave had trained Ben in search and rescue techniques, and the Border Collie was eager to put his skills to the test.

Ben and Dave hiked into the Highlands, searching for any sign of Kate. They combed through rocky terrain, crossed streams, and climbed steep hills. As they searched, Ben sniffed the air, looking for any scent that might lead them to Kate.

After several hours of searching, Ben picked up a scent. He began to lead Dave up a rocky path, his tail wagging with excitement. Dave knew that Ben had found something important, and he followed the dog's lead.

As they climbed higher, the weather grew colder and the winds picked up. But Ben was undeterred. He led Dave through a narrow pass between two mountains, and suddenly, they saw something in the distance.

It was Kate, lying on the ground, cold and exhausted. She had fallen and injured her leg, and was unable to continue hiking. But thanks to Ben's keen sense of smell, she had been found.

Dave quickly radioed for help, and a rescue team was dispatched to the area. They arrived soon after and were able to airlift Kate to safety. She was taken to a hospital, where she received medical attention for her injuries.

Ben had saved the day, and his bravery didn't go unnoticed. He was awarded the PDSA Gold Medal, one of the highest honors a civilian animal can receive. The medal recognized Ben's exceptional bravery and dedication to helping others.

But for Ben, the medal wasn't the most important thing. What mattered most was that he had helped save a life. He had used his skills and training to do something incredible, and had made a real difference in the world.

Today, Ben is still a beloved member of Dave's family. He loves to play and go on walks, just like any other Border Collie. But he's also a hero, and his bravery and dedication will always be remembered.

Ben the Border Collie proved that even an ordinary dog can do extraordinary things. With his keen sense of smell and his dedication to helping others, he was able to locate a missing hiker and save her life. And for his bravery, he was awarded the PDSA Gold Medal. Ben's story is a reminder that heroes can come in all shapes and sizes, and that even the smallest among us can make a big difference in the world.

Tara

A Hero Who Helped Save Lives

Tara was born in 2006 in the United States and was trained as a search and rescue dog. She was known for her incredible sense of smell and her ability to find people in difficult situations. In January 2010, a massive earthquake hit the country of Haiti, leaving thousands of people trapped under rubble and debris.

The earthquake caused widespread devastation, and many people were left stranded and injured. As a result, a team of rescue workers was sent to Haiti to help search for survivors. Tara and her handler, named Lorraine, were among the rescue team.

As soon as they arrived in Haiti, Tara got to work. She and Lorraine searched through the rubble for any signs of life, listening for sounds or using Tara's incredible sense of smell to locate victims. The work was grueling, and the team faced many challenges, including dangerous aftershocks and limited resources.

But Tara and the team persevered, working tirelessly to save as many people as they could. They worked for days, carefully moving through the rubble, looking for any signs of life. Finally, on the third day of their search, Tara made a remarkable discovery.

Tara had detected the scent of a person buried deep under the rubble. The team immediately began to dig, carefully removing debris piece by piece. After several hours of hard work, they finally reached the person, who was alive but badly injured. Tara had saved a life!

Over the next few days, Tara and the team continued to search for survivors, working tirelessly to bring hope to a desperate situation. And thanks to their efforts, they were able to save 12 people in total.

Tara's work in Haiti made her a hero, and she received a lot of attention and praise for her bravery. She was featured in news articles and on television shows, and people all over the world were inspired by her incredible work.

In recognition of her bravery, Tara was awarded the PDSA Gold Medal, which is one of the highest honors a dog can receive. The medal is given to animals who have shown exceptional bravery and dedication in service to humans.

Tara's story is a reminder of the incredible bond between humans and dogs. When disaster strikes, dogs like Tara are there to help, using their incredible skills and dedication to save lives. And while Tara may be gone now, her legacy lives on, inspiring new generations of search and rescue dogs to continue her work.

So next time you see a dog like Tara, remember that they are not just pets or companions, but heroes in their own right. They work hard to protect us and save lives, and we should be grateful for everything they do.

Tara was an incredible Labrador Retriever who helped save lives in the aftermath of the Haiti earthquake. Her bravery and dedication to her work made her a true hero, and she will always be remembered for her incredible service to others. Let's all take a moment to honor Tara and all the other amazing dogs who work to make the world a better place.

Blek

The Hero with a Nose for Landmines

In Bosnia and Herzegovina, there was a brave dog named Blek. Blek was a German Shepherd who worked in a K-9 unit, which meant he had a very important job to do. His job was to help locate landmines and unexploded bombs, which could be very dangerous and even deadly.

Blek lived with his human partner, a soldier named Darko. Darko and Blek had been working together for many years and had become the best of friends. They had been through a lot together, but nothing could stop them from doing their job and keeping people safe.

One day, Blek and Darko were called to a village where there had been reports of unexploded bombs. When they arrived, they saw that the village was in ruins. The buildings had been destroyed, and the people were living in tents. Darko knew that they had to act fast to find the bombs before anyone else got hurt.

Blek sniffed around the area, searching for any signs of explosives. He was very good at his job, and soon he found a spot where the ground felt different. Darko knew that this was a sign of a bomb, so he carefully dug in the ground. Sure enough, he found an unexploded bomb.

Blek and Darko continued to search the area, finding more and more bombs. It was a dangerous job, but they knew that they had to keep going to keep people safe. Blek was always one step ahead, and Darko trusted him completely.

As they were searching, they heard a noise coming from a nearby building. They cautiously approached the building, and Blek barked to let Darko know that someone was inside. They carefully entered the building and found a young girl who had been trapped under some debris. Blek had found her, and she was alive because of him.

Darko and Blek continued their search for several more days, and with each bomb they found, they knew they were saving lives. The people in the village were grateful for their hard work, and they knew that Blek was a hero.

After their work was done, Blek and Darko returned home to their families. They were both exhausted, but they knew that they had done something important. Blek had saved countless lives with his keen sense of smell, and Darko was proud to have him as his partner.

Blek went on to work on many more missions, and he became known as a hero in Bosnia and Herzegovina. His bravery and dedication to his job made him an inspiration to all who knew him.

Blek was a true hero who risked his life to save others. He was a brave dog who never gave up, even when the job was tough. Blek and Darko were a team who worked together to keep people safe, and they did an amazing job. Blek is a reminder that even the smallest actions can make a big difference and that anyone can be a hero.

Endal

*The Canine Companion Who
Changed a Veteran's Life*

Meet Endal, a special Labrador Retriever who not only became a loyal pet to his owner but also a life-changing assistant to a Gulf War veteran. Endal's story is one of courage, companionship, and determination. Let's dive into the life of this amazing dog and learn how he became a hero.

Endal was born on December 13, 1995, in Devon, England. He was raised and trained to become a service dog, a special type of canine who assists people with disabilities in performing various tasks. Endal was trained by the Canine Partners organization, which specializes in training service dogs for people with physical disabilities.

In 1999, Endal was assigned to Gulf War veteran Allen Parton, who had suffered a serious head injury in a car accident that left him unable to walk, talk, or remember his past. Parton was confined to a wheelchair and needed assistance with everyday tasks such as paying for items, turning off lights, and picking up objects. This is where Endal came in.

Endal was a natural-born helper. He was not only well-trained, but he had a special bond with Parton, which made him an excellent assistant. Endal could do many things, such as retrieving Parton's wallet from his pocket and handing it to the cashier, paying for items with a credit card machine, and even operating automatic doors.

But Endal was more than just a helper. He was also a loyal companion to Parton, who had lost all of his memories and connections to his past. Endal would stay by his side and offer him comfort and companionship, which was invaluable to Parton's well-being.

In 2001, Endal and Parton were out for a walk when Parton suddenly fell out of his wheelchair and hit his head on the pavement. Endal immediately sprang into action, pulling the emergency cord on Parton's wheelchair to call for help. He then dragged Parton onto his side to open his airway and kept him warm by lying on top of him until the paramedics arrived.

Endal's quick thinking and actions saved Parton's life that day. He was awarded the PDSA Gold Medal, the highest honor a civilian animal can receive in the United Kingdom, for his bravery and devotion to his owner.

Endal's heroism didn't stop there. He and Parton became ambassadors for Canine Partners, helping to raise awareness and funds for the organization. They traveled around the country and even met the Queen of England, who was impressed by Endal's skills and personality.

In 2008, Endal retired from service due to old age and health issues. He continued to live with Parton as a beloved pet and companion until his passing in 2009. Endal's legacy lives on, inspiring others to see the true potential of dogs as service animals and companions.

Endal's story is a testament to the power of the human-animal bond. Through his actions, he not only helped his owner but also inspired others to see the true potential of service dogs. Endal's bravery, loyalty, and determination will never be forgotten, and he will always be remembered as a true hero in the hearts of those whose lives he touched.

Endal was more than just a service dog. He was a loyal companion, a life-saver, and an inspiration to many. His story shows us that dogs are capable of amazing things and that the bond between humans and animals is truly special.

Gidget

The Little Dog with Big Ears

Meet Gidget, a tiny Chihuahua with big ears and an even bigger heart. She may be small, but she's a hero in her own right. Gidget was a hearing assistance dog, trained to help her owner, who was deaf, navigate the world with ease. Let's learn more about this little hero and how she helped her owner.

Gidget was born in 2003 in San Francisco, California. She was adopted by her owner, a woman who is deaf, when she was just a puppy. Gidget quickly bonded with her owner and became her constant companion. However, her owner faced many challenges in her daily life due to her hearing impairment.

That's when Gidget stepped in to help. She was trained as a hearing assistance dog by Canine Companions for Independence, a non-profit organization that provides assistance dogs to people with disabilities. Gidget learned to recognize and alert her owner to important sounds such as doorbells, smoke alarms, and phone rings.

Gidget was trained to touch her owner's leg with her paw to get her attention whenever she heard a sound. This way, her owner could be aware of important noises and respond accordingly. Gidget was also trained to lead her owner to the source of the sound if necessary, such as the door if someone was ringing the doorbell.

Gidget's owner was amazed at how quickly Gidget learned to respond to sounds. She was grateful for the extra help and support that Gidget provided her with. With Gidget by her side, her owner felt more confident and independent.

Gidget and her owner quickly became inseparable. They went everywhere together, whether it was running errands or going for a walk in the park. Gidget was a friendly and sociable dog, and she loved meeting new people and dogs.

Despite her small size, Gidget was a fearless protector. She would bark loudly to warn her owner if she sensed any danger, whether it was a stranger approaching or a sudden loud noise. Her owner felt safe and secure with Gidget by her side.

Gidget's adorable looks and endearing personality quickly made her a celebrity. She appeared on various TV shows and news segments, showcasing her skills as a hearing assistance dog. Her story inspired many people and raised awareness about the important role that assistance dogs play in the lives of people with disabilities.

Gidget lived a long and happy life with her owner, passing away at the age of 15 in 2018. Her owner was devastated by the loss of her beloved companion, but she knew that Gidget had given her the gift of independence and freedom. Gidget's legacy lives on, inspiring others to recognize the value and importance of assistance dogs in the lives of people with disabilities.

In conclusion, Gidget was a little dog with a big heart and an important job. She helped her owner navigate the world with ease and provided her with the extra support and assistance she needed. Gidget's story is a testament to the incredible bond between humans and their animal companions, and the powerful impact that dogs can have on our lives.

Sallie

A Brave Canine Hero of the American Civil War

Dogs are often called man's best friend, and there's a good reason for that. These furry creatures have been by our side for thousands of years, serving us in many different ways. They have been hunting companions, guard dogs, sled dogs, and even therapy animals. However, there is another role that some dogs have played in history – that of a military mascot. And one of the most famous of these mascots was Sallie, a Staffordshire Terrier who served with the 11th Pennsylvania Volunteer Infantry during the American Civil War.

The American Civil War was a time of great conflict and strife, with the Union Army and the Confederate Army fighting for control of the country. Sallie's story begins in 1861, when she was just a puppy, and was given as a gift to the 11th Pennsylvania Volunteer Infantry by a local resident of West Chester, Pennsylvania. The soldiers immediately took a liking to her, and she quickly became their mascot, accompanying them on their journey to the battlefield.

Sallie was not just a cute and cuddly companion, though. She quickly showed that she had a strong spirit and a fierce loyalty to her fellow soldiers. She would march alongside the men, wagging her tail and barking happily, and would stand guard at the front of the line during battles. She was a familiar face to the soldiers, and they all loved her.

During the Battle of Cedar Mountain in 1862, Sallie's bravery was put to the test. The Confederate Army was advancing, and the Union soldiers were in danger of being overrun. Sallie, sensing the danger, ran to the front of the line and barked fiercely at the enemy soldiers, distracting them and buying the

Union soldiers precious time. Her actions allowed the Union soldiers to regroup and repel the Confederate Army's attack. Sallie was hailed as a hero, and the soldiers knew that they had a true friend and companion in her.

After the Battle of Cedar Mountain, Sallie became even more beloved by the soldiers of the 11th Pennsylvania Volunteer Infantry. She was given a special collar that read "Sallie, 11th PA" and was allowed to march at the head of the line during parades. She was even given her own drummer, who would play a special tune whenever Sallie was present.

Sallie's bravery and loyalty did not go unnoticed by the enemy soldiers, either. During the Battle of Gettysburg, Confederate soldiers captured Sallie and took her to their camp. The soldiers taunted her and tried to make her bark, but she remained silent, refusing to give away the Union soldiers' position. Eventually, the Union soldiers were able to rescue Sallie, and she was returned to her rightful place with the 11th Pennsylvania Volunteer Infantry.

Sallie continued to serve with the 11th Pennsylvania Volunteer Infantry until the Battle of Hatcher's Run in 1865. During the battle, Sallie was hit by enemy fire and killed. The soldiers were devastated by her loss and buried her on the battlefield, marking her grave with a special stone that read "Sallie, a Brave Heroine of the Civil War."

Today, Sallie's memory lives on. The stone marking her grave was moved to the Gettysburg National Military Park, where it can still be seen today. In addition, a bronze statue of Sallie was erected at the park, depicting her standing guard at the front of the line, just as she did during battles.

Sallie's legacy is not just one of bravery and loyalty, but also of the important role that dogs have played in history.

Rags

The Brave Stray Dog of WW1

Long ago, in a world at war, a little stray dog found his way into the heart of an American soldier. His name was Rags, and he was a terrier mix with a scruffy brown coat and bright eyes that shone with intelligence.

Rags had been wandering the streets of Paris, searching for scraps of food and a place to sleep, when he stumbled upon the soldier, Private James

Donovan. Donovan was a young man from Connecticut who had joined the United States Army to fight in World War I. He was stationed in France and had just returned from the front lines, where he had witnessed the horrors of war.

When Donovan saw Rags, he felt an instant connection. The little dog was dirty and thin, but he had a friendly demeanor and a wagging tail. Donovan took pity on him and decided to adopt him as his own. He cleaned him up, fed him, and gave him a warm place to sleep. From that day on, Rags was Donovan's loyal companion, and the two were inseparable.

Donovan soon discovered that Rags was no ordinary dog. He was smart, fearless, and had a keen sense of smell. He could detect the faintest scent of danger and would alert Donovan to any nearby enemy troops or incoming artillery fire. Rags proved to be an invaluable asset to Donovan and his fellow soldiers, and he quickly became a beloved mascot of the 1st Infantry Division.

Rags accompanied Donovan and his unit as they fought in some of the bloodiest battles of the war. He was there at Chateau-Thierry, Belleau Wood, and the Argonne Forest. In the trenches, Rags would comfort the soldiers, snuggling up to them for warmth and licking their wounds. He would even carry messages from one end of the battlefield to the other, dodging bullets and artillery fire with astonishing agility.

But Rags' greatest act of heroism occurred during a gas attack in September 1918. The Germans had unleashed a deadly cloud of chlorine gas, which could cause blindness, suffocation, and death. The American soldiers were caught off guard, and many of them were choking and gasping for air. Donovan, who had been wounded in the attack, was lying unconscious on the ground.

Rags, however, was not affected by the gas. He sprang into action, running back and forth between the wounded soldiers, barking and nipping at their uniforms to get their attention. He even pulled Donovan by his sleeve, dragging him to safety. Thanks to Rags' bravery, many lives were saved that day.

After the war, Donovan and Rags returned to the United States, where they were greeted as heroes. Rags was awarded the rank of sergeant, and Donovan was awarded the Distinguished Service Cross for his bravery. They traveled the country, visiting schools and hospitals, and inspiring others with their courage and loyalty.

Sadly, Rags' health began to decline as he aged. He had been exposed to gas during the war, and it had weakened his lungs. In 1936, Rags passed away at the age of 20. He was buried with full military honors, and a monument was erected in his honor at the Rock Island Arsenal Museum in Illinois.

Today, Rags' legacy lives on, as a symbol of the bravery and sacrifice of the millions of animals who have served alongside humans in times of war. He was a true hero, a dog who gave everything he had to protect his beloved owner and his fellow soldiers.

Bosco

The Joyful Golden Retriever Who Brings Smiles to Kids' Faces

Bosco is a very special Golden Retriever who has a very important job. He works at a hospice for children with life-limiting conditions. His job is to bring joy and comfort to the children and their families. And he does his job very well!

Bosco is a very friendly and outgoing dog. He loves people and he especially loves kids. When he arrives at the hospice, he greets everyone with a wagging tail and a big smile on his face. The kids love him immediately and they can't wait to play with him.

Bosco's job is to be a therapy dog. A therapy dog is a specially trained dog that helps people feel better. Therapy dogs visit hospitals, nursing homes, schools, and other places where people might need some extra love and attention.

Bosco's training as a therapy dog began when he was just a puppy. His owner, Mary, knew that he had a very special personality and would be perfect for this kind of work. So she enrolled him in a training program where he learned how to be calm and gentle around people, how to follow commands, and how to be a good listener.

Now, Bosco visits the hospice twice a week. He spends time with the kids, playing games, cuddling, and just being a friend. Bosco is very intuitive, so he knows when a child needs extra attention or a gentle touch. He's always there to offer a paw or a lick, and he's always ready to listen.

One of Bosco's favorite things to do at the hospice is to play ball with the kids. He has a special ball that he brings with him, and the kids love to toss it back and forth with him. Sometimes they even have races to see who can get the ball first.

Bosco also loves to give hugs. He's a big dog, so he can wrap his paws around a child and give them a big, warm hug. The kids love it, and it always brings a smile to their face.

But Bosco's job is not just to bring joy to the kids. He also helps the parents and the staff at the hospice. Seeing their children happy and relaxed makes a huge difference in their day. And the staff members love to see the positive effect that Bosco has on the kids.

Bosco is a very popular dog at the hospice. The kids all know his name and they look forward to his visits. He's like a rockstar! And he loves the attention. But he also knows when it's time to be calm and quiet. He's very respectful of the kids' needs and he never gets too rowdy or too loud.

Bosco has made a big difference in the lives of many children and their families. He's a reminder that even in the toughest of times, there can still be joy and happiness. And he's a reminder that sometimes, all you need is a friend to help you through.

Bosco is not just a therapy dog, he's also a member of the hospice family. He's loved by everyone who knows him, and he's made a big impact on the lives of many. He's a true hero, and we're lucky to have him in our community.

So next time you see a Golden Retriever, think of Bosco and all the joy and happiness he brings to the kids at the hospice. And if you're lucky enough to meet a therapy dog like Bosco, be sure to give them a pat on the head and say thank you for all the hard work they do. They're truly amazing animals!

Leo

The Pit Bull Who Saved His Family

Leo the Pit Bull may look tough and strong, but he's also a hero! Leo saved his family from a house fire and became a national sensation for his bravery.

Leo was just like any other dog, living a happy life with his family. His owners, the McPhersons, loved him and he loved them back. Leo had always been protective of his family and would do anything to keep them safe.

One night, while the McPhersons were fast asleep, Leo smelled something strange. It was a faint smell, but it was enough to wake him up. Leo knew something was wrong, and he immediately ran to his owners' room and started barking loudly.

At first, the McPhersons were annoyed at Leo for waking them up in the middle of the night. But then they realized that Leo was trying to tell them something important. They followed Leo to the front door and saw that smoke was billowing out from under the door.

The McPhersons were terrified. They had to get out of the house immediately. They didn't know what to do until Leo stepped up to help. Leo led them to a window and they climbed out with his help. It was a good thing that Leo was strong and sturdy, because he was able to hold on to his owners and make sure they got out safely.

Once they were outside, the McPhersons called the fire department. They watched as their house went up in flames, but they were just grateful to be alive. Leo saved their lives, and they couldn't thank him enough.

Leo quickly became a national sensation. People from all over the country heard about his heroic act, and he was even featured on TV and in newspapers. Everyone wanted to meet Leo and give him a big hug. Leo's owners were happy that he was getting so much attention, but they knew that he was just being himself. He was a loyal and protective dog who loved his family.

Leo didn't let his newfound fame go to his head. He was still the same loving and loyal dog that he had always been. He continued to protect his family, and they continued to love him.

Leo's story is a reminder that dogs are more than just pets. They are members of our families and they will do anything to keep us safe. Leo's heroic act saved his owners' lives, and he will always be remembered as a brave and loyal dog.

Leo's story also reminds us that pit bulls are often misunderstood. Many people think that they are dangerous dogs, but that's not true at all. Pit bulls can be loving and loyal pets, just like any other breed of dog. Leo's bravery is proof of that.

Leo is a true hero and a reminder that dogs are more than just pets. They are our friends, our protectors, and our family members. We should always treat them with love and respect, just like they do for us.

So the next time you see a dog, whether it's a pit bull or any other breed, remember Leo's story. Remember that they are more than just pets. They are heroes, and they deserve our love and respect.

Toby

The Hero Who Smelled Danger

Meet Toby, the brave and smart Golden Retriever who helped save his owner's life by alerting her to a gas leak in their home. Toby is a loving and loyal dog who always looks out for his family. One day, Toby's owner, Sarah, was feeling sick and decided to take a nap. Little did she know, danger was lurking in her home.

Toby noticed a strange smell in the air and started to bark and whine uncontrollably. Sarah woke up to Toby's frantic barking and immediately noticed the gas smell too. She quickly realized that Toby was trying to warn her of a gas leak in the house.

Without hesitation, Sarah grabbed Toby and rushed out of the house to safety. She called the gas company, and they confirmed that there was indeed a gas leak in the house. Thanks to Toby's alertness and quick action, Sarah and her family were safe from a potentially deadly situation.

Sarah was amazed by Toby's bravery and intelligence. She realized that he truly is a hero and decided to share his story with the world. She posted a picture of Toby on social media with the caption "Meet my hero, Toby! He saved my life today by alerting me to a gas leak in our home. I am so grateful to have him in my life."

Toby's story quickly went viral, and he became a local celebrity. People from all over the world were inspired by his bravery and intelligence. Toby even got invited to appear on a talk show, where he was interviewed about his heroic act.

During the interview, Toby's trainer explained how he had been trained to detect the scent of gas. Golden Retrievers have a strong sense of smell and are often used as detection dogs. Toby's trainer had trained him to recognize the scent of gas and alert his owner by barking and whining.

Toby's trainer also explained that it's important for all pet owners to be aware of the signs of a gas leak in their home. The signs include a hissing sound, a rotten egg smell, and dead plants or vegetation around the gas line. If you suspect a gas leak in your home, it's important to evacuate immediately and call the gas company.

After the interview, Toby became even more popular. People from all over the world started sending him gifts and letters, thanking him for his bravery. Toby's owner, Sarah, was overwhelmed by the support and love that Toby was receiving.

Toby continued to live his life as a hero and a beloved family pet. He loved to play fetch, go for walks, and cuddle with his family. His heroism had made him even more beloved by his family and friends.

Toby's story is a reminder of the importance of having a pet in our lives. Pets are not only great companions, but they can also save our lives in times of danger. It's important to take good care of our pets and to appreciate them for the love and joy they bring into our lives.

In conclusion, Toby is a true hero who saved his owner's life by alerting her to a gas leak in their home. His bravery and intelligence have inspired people from all over the world. Toby's story is a reminder of the importance of having a pet in our lives and the love and joy they bring into our lives.

Xanto

The Canine Police Officer

Have you ever heard of a dog that works as a police officer? It might sound strange, but it's true! In Italy, there was a brave German Shepherd named Xanto who worked as a police dog and helped the police catch criminals and find missing people. Let's learn more about this amazing dog!

Xanto was born in Germany and was trained to work as a police dog. He was trained to track people, find hidden things, and protect his handler. His incredible sense of smell, hearing, and sight made him an ideal police dog.

When Xanto was just a year old, he was sent to Italy to join the Italian police force. There, he was partnered with a police officer named Cristian. Cristian and Xanto quickly became best friends and worked together to keep the people of Italy safe.

One of Xanto's first jobs was to help the police catch a group of burglars who were robbing houses in the area. Xanto was able to track the scent of the burglars and lead the police straight to their hiding spot. Thanks to Xanto's help, the burglars were caught and taken to jail.

Another time, Xanto was called in to help find a little boy who had gone missing in the woods. The boy had wandered away from his family, and the police were worried he might be lost or hurt. Xanto used his incredible sense of smell to track the boy's scent through the woods. After a few hours of searching, Xanto led Cristian and the other police officers straight to the boy. The little boy was scared, but thanks to Xanto, he was safe and sound.

Xanto wasn't just good at catching criminals and finding missing people - he was also trained to protect his handler. One time, Cristian was trying to arrest a suspect who was resisting arrest. The suspect started to attack Cristian, but Xanto was there to protect him. Xanto barked and growled at the suspect, scaring him away and keeping Cristian safe.

Xanto was so good at his job that he received several awards for his service. He was awarded the Gold Medal of Valor, which is the highest honor a police dog can receive in Italy. Xanto was also given a special vest to wear that protected him from bullets and knives. This vest helped keep Xanto safe while he was working to protect the people of Italy.

Despite all of his hard work, Xanto still loved to play and have fun. He enjoyed chasing after toys and playing tug-of-war with Cristian. He also loved to be petted and cuddled, just like any other dog.

Xanto's story shows us just how incredible dogs can be. They are intelligent, brave, and loyal creatures that can help keep us safe. Xanto's work as a police dog is a great example of how dogs can be trained to do amazing things. Xanto will always be remembered as a hero in Italy, and his legacy will continue to inspire people all over the world.

In conclusion, Xanto was an amazing German Shepherd who served as a police dog in Italy. He helped catch criminals, find missing people, and protect his handler. Xanto's bravery and loyalty will always be remembered, and his story is a testament to just how incredible dogs can be.

Hooch

The French Mastiff Who Saved His Owner's Life

In the quiet neighborhood of Oakwood, a French Mastiff named Hooch lived with his owner, Mr. Johnson. Hooch was a big and strong dog with a heart of gold. He loved nothing more than spending time with his owner and playing fetch in the backyard. But one fateful night, Hooch's bravery and loyalty were put to the test when an intruder broke into their home.

Mr. Johnson was fast asleep when he heard a loud noise coming from the living room. He got out of bed and walked to the door, only to find a masked man holding a knife. The intruder had broken into their house with the intention of stealing valuables, but when he saw Mr. Johnson, he became violent and attacked him.

As Mr. Johnson struggled to defend himself, Hooch heard the commotion and quickly sprang into action. The French Mastiff charged towards the attacker, barking and growling fiercely. The intruder, taken aback by the sudden appearance of the massive dog, hesitated for a moment, giving Mr. Johnson just enough time to escape and call for help.

The intruder, however, was not willing to give up so easily. He swung his knife at Hooch, hoping to scare him off. But the brave dog did not back down. With all his might, Hooch lunged forward and bit the intruder's arm, causing him to drop the knife. The intruder then fled, leaving Hooch and Mr. Johnson unharmed but shaken by the experience.

Thanks to Hooch's bravery and loyalty, Mr. Johnson was able to survive the home invasion. Hooch had risked his own life to protect his owner, and for that, Mr. Johnson was forever grateful. From that day on, Hooch became more than just a pet to Mr. Johnson - he became a true hero and a loyal companion.

After the incident, Hooch received a lot of attention and praise from the local community. People admired his bravery and loyalty, and many wanted to meet the courageous dog. But Hooch remained humble and continued to live his life as he always had - playing fetch, lounging in the sun, and spending time with his beloved owner.

Despite the danger he had faced, Hooch remained a gentle and friendly dog. He loved nothing more than cuddling with Mr. Johnson and showering him with kisses. But when it came down to protecting his owner, Hooch was a fierce warrior, ready to defend him with all his might.

In the years that followed, Hooch continued to serve as a loyal companion to Mr. Johnson. He accompanied him on walks, snuggled with him on the couch, and guarded their home with vigilance. But even though Hooch was no longer called upon to defend his owner from intruders, his bravery and loyalty remained an inspiration to all who knew him.

Hooch's story is a testament to the incredible bond between humans and animals. Hooch may have been just a dog, but to Mr. Johnson, he was so much more than that. He was a friend, a protector, and a hero. And though Hooch may be gone, his memory will live on forever in the hearts of those who loved him.

Thanks for reading this book filled with inspiring, true stories about Man's Best Friend.

If you enjoyed the book, we would greatly appreciate it if you could take a moment to leave a review on Amazon. Your review will help others to discover this book and join in the fun! Thank you again for joining us on this wild and wacky journey of discovery!

— *Anthony Ripley*

Made in the USA
Las Vegas, NV
08 November 2024